PRAISE FOR JACQUELINE PIRTLE

"Jacqueline takes you always directly to what you are ready to see or experience."

— LONGTIME CLIENT AND READER

"It is liberating to face your own blocks and to be finally free of the weight that they have caused for many years. And while for me the changes I'm experiencing are noticeable and real, I still feel like myself. Just a more sure self."

— LONGTIME CLIENT AND READER

"Jacqueline makes me BELIEVE I can be and live a joyful and magical existence every new day of my life!"

— LONGTIME CLIENT AND READER

The *365 Days of Happiness* bestselling author

JACQUELINE PIRTLE

BRAGGING

Because you're worth it!

THE EXTENDED EDITION

COPYRIGHT

Copyright © 2021 Jacqueline Pirtle
www.FreakyHealer.com

All rights reserved. No part of this book may be reproduced or transmitted in any form or by any means, electronic or mechanical, including photocopying, recording, or by any information storage and retrieval system without the written permission of the publisher, except where permitted by law.

ISBN-13: 978-1-955059-19-0

Publisher: Freaky Healer

Editor-in-chief: Zoe Pirtle
All-round Support: Mitch Pirtle

Book cover design by Kingwood Creations kingwoodcreations.com

Author photo courtesy of Lionel Madiou madious.com

I want to let you know that all my books and holistic practitioner work together, as a wholesome system, are supporting you to live a more conscious, mindful, and happier life.

However, I made it so you can receive the benefit of living more joyously solely by working through this terrific journal book, while also experiencing the full satisfaction in continuing on to the next journal of this series—not to mention the rock solid tools you get by reading any of my other books or adding in my podcast *The Daily Freak*. Either way, I know you'll love my inspirational teachings.

Find out more at:
FreakyHealer.com
Amazon - Jacqueline Pirtle's Author Page
The Daily Freak Podcast

Before you dive in, I want to thank you for hopping on the magic train with me! I truly hope you enjoy *Bragging* as much as I loved writing it, and if you do, it would be wonderful if you could take a short minute and leave a review on Amazon and Goodreads.com as soon as you can.

Your kind feedback helps other readers find my books more easily, and to be happy faster. Consider it a joy-deed for the world.

Thank you!

ACKNOWLEDGMENTS

Let's be honest here… I have a dream team!

I could not have finished this book without the help of talented, creative, high-for-life, and phenomenal professionals.

From the bottom of my heart, I want to thank Zoe Pirtle for her editorial mastery; Mitch Pirtle for his all-round support; kingwoodcreations.com for their fun and polished book cover design; and madiouART.com for an amazing photo shoot.

I'd also like to extend a huge "Thank You!" to all fans of my work and books—I created this beautiful journal series for you.

Life is spectacular with you on my side!

BE the self-bragger you are meant to be!

DEDICATION

I dedicate this journal to all those thinking that bragging is hard, or not OK, and challenge them to make bragging their lifestyle!

INTRODUCTION

Proud bragger,

It is high-time for this journal to exist—a bragging, gloating, gushing, and filling-your-pride-to-the-brim kind of workbook.

I'm over the moon happy to say, "Here it is!"

It is also long overdue to put a stop to all misunderstandings and negative meanings about the *art of aligned bragging* or being in love with oneself and life to the extent of behaving in a manner of feeling full of oneself.

How much better can it get than someone showing up as the best version of themselves and the most self-loving ever, when as a matter of fact, everything is *ONE* and the same energy, always connected and sharing at all times—meaning that they share and spread their boasting happy self with everything and everyone and are uplifting the whole world because of it?

I say nothing else is better than that—for them and for all!

Sure, misaligned bragging exists and that version of gloating never feels good, but what we are focusing on in this journal is the aligned boasting which feels incredible and is what everyone is here - in physicality - to choose, and also to enjoy.

INTRODUCTION

So how amazing is it that, by living through the naturally well-feeling bragging ways that you are about to create in this journal, you will spread your love for yourself and your life - and the fun that you are having - to everything and everyone, lifting the whole world into a higher state, or at least as high as your surroundings want to go with you?

I say that's pretty cool!

Bragging helps you to overcome your old habits of selling yourself short while inspiring you to dream big, then even bigger, and to feel your own personal power everywhere and at anytime —inviting you to go for the best of the best at all times.

There, an ocean of opportunities will catch hold of you, inviting you to dive deep. Just think of that incredible match-up and shift into the higher frequency of bliss, by being *ONE* with the excitement of living a fun life filled with incredible manifestations.

A bragging way of life gives your best version of you the spotlight—all while changing at a constant and vivid speed, in flow with how life naturally happens. I'm inspired to think that this is what you really want and who you truly are here to BE and live as.

Journaling through this 90 day extended edition of ***Bragging*** brings huge calibrations into the equation so you can experience life like you never have before, craft a time beyond your expectations, and love what you live—to the extent of becoming a master in living consciously and mindfully, feeling phenomenal while manifesting the best of the best.

It's a change that is forever!

As a side note, there are a couple of bonus days at the end in case you ever find the need to do two in a day, or so you can keep working while you wait for the next journal in this series to arrive. I also left you a few blank **bragging** pages to journal about deepening your ways of being proudly alive.

INTRODUCTION

Enough chit-chat, I know you are ready—so grab your pen and have incredible fun with catching more life than you have ever caught, in your new crazy ways.

Happiest,
    Jacqueline

Day 1

IMAGINE yourself behind closed doors - not locked - and even though you are in a comfy and cozy room, you have a sense of limitation, of being tucked away and not as free as you could be. You are grateful being in such a wonderful room, but deep inside you know that behind those doors is a way of being YOU that is so much more than you are now—more colorful, fun, inspired, and more alive. Simply *more*! If you only could just sneak a little peek, or even better, say "YES!" to going through those doors. Out of the blue you decide, "I'm going for it! I'm taking my chances!" How does this feel—now that you have made the decision to go for *more* in life, and *more* as you? Get your more-experience on paper and be ready, because tomorrow you will make the majestic leap into your new way of living your free and bragging life.

___
___
___
___
___
___
___
___
___
___
___
___
___
___

Bragging - Because you're worth it!

 ay 2

FILLED to the brim with excitement of your thrilling decision to fly higher than you have ever before say, "I can't wait!" and grab those door handles with your willing hands. Start turning the knobs, while feeling that your true adventure awaits and knowing it will be one of a kind! Keep at it until the doors spring open—embracing you with an invitation to walk through. With a smile and a deep breath, and in a knowing trance, you start your essential walk jam-packed with the understanding that your inner being is guiding and pulling you towards your best life ever. Go on, this is your glorious tunnel of freedom in which you walk to liberate yourself, leaving all chains from your old ways behind. With every forward-step you take your gorgeous tunnel brightens and you feel lighter than ever. Prepare yourself for the brightest show to be at the end of your walk of liberty; the entrance into your new bragging life! How does your freedom feel? Journal, liberator, journal!

Get excited because tomorrow, your arrival in your new world of being *outside those doors* and showing up fully as you is the main attraction.

_____
_____
_____
_____
_____
_____
_____

Bragging - Because you're worth it!

 ay 3

PEEKABOO! Open your eyes and realize that today is the day where you made it—home! You took a chance, you walked the walk, now here you are. You have arrived in your perfect world for you—where you are your true you and will brag all the way to the millions of stars about yourself and your life, because after all, that is what you came here to do in this journal and in your life. You came to be so full of yourself and so sure about yourself that insecurities, criticism, or denials - yours or anybody else's - are jobless and can't exist. How does this feel, to be freely you? Are you exited to start bragging with pride? How much do you love, respect, accept, appreciate, and thank yourself in this new world—and will you go all out to do it more? Write, beautiful new bragger, write!

Tomorrow we'll get rid of the negative old beliefs attached to bragging—but today you need not worry at all. Instead, you'll brag for, and about, yourself without any limits.

_____
_____
_____
_____
_____
_____
_____
_____
_____
_____
_____

Bragging - Because you're worth it!

 ay 4

LET'S burry the downer meanings of bragging!

Think about the energy that the word *bragging* comes with—a feeling of security and sureness, knowing yourself, and being a big, huge, and humongous person; but it's also uplifting and fun-spilling. It shows respect, appreciation, acceptance, gratitude, and love for youself—while seeing a bigger life and purpose, and the ability and willingness to BE more and live more. What a powerful energy! Write about the beautiful meanings that bragging has for you - now that the old nonsense and negativity is straightened out - and list your newfound expectations for yourself and your life.

_____
_____
_____
_____
_____
_____
_____
_____
_____
_____
_____
_____
_____
_____
_____
_____

Bragging - Because you're worth it!

 ay 5

BRAGGING REPRESENTS your pride for yourself and shows how much fun you are actually having in your life—even more potently, how much phenomenal-ness you are open to allow-in for yourself. Let's start with pride today—we will tackle *fun, being open, and allowing-in* over the next few days. Go deep into what being proud of yourself really means to you! Is it self-love, letting go of traumas and pains, and being freer than you have ever been? Journal, proud one, journal!

Bragging - Because you're worth it!

 ay 6

How much fun do you really have in life, and how much more of it do you want? What could bragging about yourself have to do with getting bliss into your life more often? Would gushing about your gorgeous heart - how big it is - and your grand love it holds be of fun-value? Or could bragging about your talent of being a flamenco dancer - while in truth you can't dance to save your life - be a fun thing to enjoy? How will you create an unlimited amount of joy, giggles, and laughter in your new world?

_____
_____
_____
_____
_____
_____
_____
_____
_____
_____
_____
_____
_____
_____
_____
_____
_____
_____
_____
_____

Bragging - Because you're worth it!

 ay 7

You have to be an open-minded, open-hearted, open-worded, and open-hearing, open-feeling, open-tasting, open-smelling, and open-to-everything-in-life kind of person in order to be a bragger who loves to brag—not to mention being on the light side of life to not take everything so seriously. Why? Because all else puts roadblocks in your way by giving you excuses not to gloat about yourself and your life. So, how open can you be - or become - to really, really fly high as your own personal bragger?

_____
_____
_____
_____
_____
_____
_____
_____
_____
_____
_____
_____
_____
_____
_____
_____
_____
_____

Bragging - Because you're worth it!

 ay 8

ALLOWING yourself to stand on the highest pedestal - or at least five stacked high - and feel amazing for yourself is the master golden key to living a great life, besides being the portal to let wonderfulness in. So allow yourself to brag about your amazingness! But wowzers there is so much more; shouting out to the whole world that you are incredible - not that the world *needs* to know since all that matters is your unshakable inner knowing - brightens the globe with your undeniable shiner abilities and incredible essence of light. Are you that allowing? How much higher will you allow yourself to go, and what more do you want for yourself?

Bragging - Because you're worth it!

ay 9

LET'S talk about the action of bragging since most would love to brag a little - or a lot - more and it's time to come out of the shame-room and see the art of bragging about yourself and your life in a new and truthful light. When you brag, you love yourself, you are standing in and up for yourself, and you are designing and also creating good - actually the best - for yourself—aside from aligning with the true worth that you really are. How will you practice your biggest and boldest bragging action yet?

___

Bragging - Because you're worth it!

 ay 10

BRAGGING IS VERY personal and is asking for a laser sharp focus on yourself, and only on yourself! Looking left or right at the world, or others, can get you back into your cozy room behind those doors—because not everyone has discovered the fun of bragging yet, and the old stigma of *being over the top is bad* still exists in physicality. The best way to get the hang of gloating is to make it a private matter at first. So without saying anything to anyone, start bragging to yourself about yourself and your life— once rooted in this fun way of living, you can take it with sureness further into the world. What are you going to brag about first, and then after?

Bragging - Because you're worth it!

 ay 11

BEING a professional bragger means that you are blessing others and the whole world into a higher frequency because you shift to BE and live in a heightened way when you gloat—given that your bragging comes from your pure heart. Everything is energy - the same energy - and constantly connected, sharing and spreading their energy. See, you uplift everything and everyone by loving yourself so much that you have to say something. I say, keep bragging even more!

Bragging - Because you're worth it!

 ay 12

WHY DO others get upset when you brag? By showing the world how much you love yourself and your life you highlight how little others love themselves and enjoy their lives. You shine a light onto how much more everyone could BE and live, and how much more fun life could be, digging up their shortcomings of living and blowing old beliefs into nothing-ness. You are outshining them! It's like one bulb being brighter than the other—but even if the brighter bulb would be dimmed, it would not make the other lighter. Never dim your bragging. Instead, keep giving them hints to brag too since only they can shine their light brighter. Your bragging is a brightening gift to the world—how will you manage that?

_____
_____
_____
_____
_____
_____
_____
_____
_____
_____
_____
_____
_____
_____
_____

Bragging - Because you're worth it!

 ay 13

BRAGGING IS DONE BEST when you are aligned with your inner being - with who you really are - and fully in the sense of what is best for you and feels fitting, so that the bragging is believable. If your gloating is impure, or your bragging is about being better than others, it will be of an un-well feeling nature—which is not the way to go. How can you stay on top of making this about you, and only you?

___

Bragging - Because you're worth it!

# Day 14

FEELING your bragging and what you are bragging about is a must in order to get the whole benefit of this wonderful way of living. Brag, but then also stop to breathe and feel how upwards shifted you sense yourself by gloating without remorse. Remember, it is an art to brag; treat it as a conscious and mindful practice of being you. How will you do that?

Bragging - Because you're worth it!

 ay 15

SEEING YOUR BRAGGING, the bragging that is always present, and everything that is there to brag about is a visionary gift that you must claim—and that your eyes want to give you the enjoyment of. So use those peepers and see bold and high! What do you see?

Bragging - Because you're worth it!

 ay 16

THINKING ABOUT YOUR BRAGGING CONSCIOUSLY, while giggling about the *more* of you that is showing up to the world, is worth the experiment of bragging the biggest and boldest ever. Be prepared for the awe of what such a gushing can achieve, the life it will create, and the wellness you are invited to indulge in. Go experiment, bragger, then journal about your wisdom!

Bragging - Because you're worth it!

 ay 17

SMELLING and tasting what bragging represents for you will let you enter a culinary phenomenal-ness—since these two senses are important to live your life. So why not go out of your old ways and into what bragging foods and drinks are for you? List please! Then devour them with a bragging "mmm" and "ahh," while noticing with amusement how the world reacts to your enjoying.

___

Bragging - Because you're worth it!

Day 18

HEAR YOURSELF BRAG, and notice the up-lifted and huge energy you become when you are in your gushing action. Listen to the birds and all of nature, giving you a free crash course in how to gloat—just think of the impressive little bee. Be aware of the bragging motorcycle and such—inspiring you to go big too. Catch what's there, incredible bragger!

Bragging - Because you're worth it!

# Day 19

"TODAY IS THE BEST DAY EVER!" Now *that* is some high-for-life bragging right there—meaning that today, you will brag the best way ever. So what will you say? What will you gloat about? Can you go even better? Today, tomorrow, and then every day after? Brag big, journaler!

___

Bragging - Because you're worth it!

 ay 20

WHENEVER YOU FEEL LOW, all you have to do is brag and immediately you will feel high and higher. It's an all-by-yourself-superpower! Initiating your bragging while alone in front of a mirror works well—start bragging, look at your bragging self, and give it a nice applause. Or rip open your front door and go out into the world—to brag and then brag some more about yourself, your life, and all that is there to brag about. Bragging about other people, your kids, partner, and family is a regal and uplifting action too—but best done only after you have fulfilled your own self-bragging job. What's your favorite way here?

___

Bragging - Because you're worth it!

 ay 21

BRAGGERS ARE CHOOSERS! Choosers are powerful! Powerful is in your nature! When you brag you choose to feel amazing and that is sheer mighty-ness because it means you understand that you are fully responsible for how you feel and how you live your life —and that no matter what, you can always shift to experience everything in a better way. What are you choosing to brag about? And how do you feel being so high up?

_____
_____
_____

Bragging - Because you're worth it!

 ay 22

"What's to brag about?" you might ask. Well, there is your breath, heart, organs, or skin that are worth a gloat. There is your physics - even if it's your pinky toe - that are excellent bragging partners. Plus, there's your inner being that is always bragging about you, so why not brag back a little? Gush about your clothes and all the material physical life things—they are not to be forgotten. How about nature, surprising you every day with different weather, animals, conditions, colors, and learning—very worth boasting about, especially when telling a story of wading through strong wind, hail, or rain to get home safely. That's being a true champion! Then there are others that love to be bragged about—you get that high essence too, since everyone always shares their energies with everything. Bragging is a powerful and uplifting practice—best thing is, you can always choose to boast at all times.

_____
_____
_____
_____
_____
_____
_____
_____
_____
_____
_____
_____

Bragging - Because you're worth it!

 ay 23

Fun fact is, that in every new split second everything is always new—and that includes you, too! It's the normal way of how life works, meaning that you can always brag anew and anew. So no matter if you just bragged about something a second ago, a new second just arrived and your new bragging can take shape. Have some fun here and unless it gets on your nerves, what's the big deal of re-bragging, especially when what you are gloating about is of such glorious nature?

Bragging - Because you're worth it!

 ay 24

How would a bragging song sound to you? What words would it include? No need to be a singer or songwriter, just go for it and produce your "I'm a bragger!" song—then belt it, baby! Don't forget to invite your loved ones.

___

Bragging - Because you're worth it!

 ay 25

WHEN YOU MEET ANOTHER BRAGGER, what is your first reaction? Is it annoyance—about their bragging or their sureness about themselves? Are you filled with pain and sadness in your own heart because you are back in your comfy room behind closed doors? Are you inspired and fired up by their energy—filling yourself and bragging higher too, since there is never anything wrong with latching onto such a heightening energy? What is your response? Become aware, while never forgetting that your reaction will naturally always be different. Your awareness is what we are hinting at here!

___

Bragging - Because you're worth it!

 Day 26

COME up with an elevator pitch of how to brag about yourself and your life in 3 minutes—your catching brag life story that tells who you are and the boasting force you bring to the table. Create a different one for work, home, being a parent or partner, and one for everyday or special days. Use your finest bragging styles here!

Bragging - Because you're worth it!

Day 27

WHEN WAS the last time you bragged about your physical body and your health? No matter the state you are in right now, you have to start somewhere. Best is to find the most boastable part, then start saying things like, " I have the strongest body ever," or "I am the smartest person I know," or "my lungs breathe the most powerful air in and out." Do this privately until you are rooted as such—then, take it public and even further and don't forget to shout it into the universe with delight. You will be amazed at how your physical well-being can change with speed by utilizing such a gloating practice—makes sense because, after all, you are filling every single cell of your whole being with powerful energy. It can't get any better than that—list your parts please!

_____
_____
_____
_____
_____
_____
_____
_____
_____
_____
_____
_____
_____
_____
_____
_____

Bragging - Because you're worth it!

 ay 28

HAVE you ever noticed a teeny tiny bird singing from the top of its lungs—soundly, loudly, and not to be missed? That is boasting at its best, staring you in the face. It really couldn't get any clearer. Do the same! Be that bird—not to be overlooked or under-heard. How will you do that?

___

Bragging - Because you're worth it!

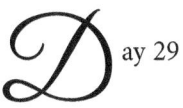 ay 29

PAIN IS WORTH BRAGGING ABOUT, but only to yourself since most individuals do not gloat about the gold that can come from pain! It goes something like this; "Wow, my back pain is of immense power and wisdom, such strong force of nature showing me what's so heavy on me lately," or; "My headache asks the world of me in such a fantastic way—to take ruthlessly better care of myself," and; "My vertigo shows me strongly how dizzy I am with my alignment. I better take this thriving sign and listen to it." You see, every symptom is the language of your physical body to communicate what exactly it is that you need to do for yourself. Worth a bragging moment, don't you think?

___

Bragging - Because you're worth it!

 ay 30

WHAT ARE your deepest wishes and desires right now? Make your glorious list! Then come up with bragging ways, words, actions, thoughts, and feelings that support what you fancy so much. Go over-gloating here—after all, you want to shift yourself into the frequency of your highest cravings.

Bragging - Because you're worth it!

 ay 31

IMAGINE yourself going a couple steps up on a ladder to look around—everything will look a little different than when you were on the ground. Take a few more steps further upwards and stop to look now—even more different of a sight. Go even higher up, just to see another variation of your surroundings. Bragging works the same way! Start to brag a little, and you'll find life being a little different than when you were behind closed doors. Brag even more and you'll get an even more enchanted time— keep bragging with a stronger vividness and guess what? Your life becomes more vivid. Soon enough you'll find yourself addicted to living as the self-knowing, self-centered, and self-loving being you have become—besides enjoying your higher fun surroundings immensely. Know that all un-charming sayings about being a bragging brat are un-true, hence, you are having more fun than ever. So where are you on your bragging-ladder?

_____
_____
_____
_____
_____
_____
_____
_____
_____
_____
_____
_____

Bragging - Because you're worth it!

 ay 32

LOVING yourself and bragging about yourself are barometers for each other. Love yourself fully and you can brag about yourself fully—love yourself barely, and that makes it hard to brag freely. As to which one should come first - to self-love or to self-brag - I leave that up to you since it's a personal chicken-and-egg dilemma. How much do you love yourself? How easy is it to brag about yourself? How much more can you love yourself—and how much more can you brag about yourself? Which one will you intensify first—your love, or your brag?

Bragging - Because you're worth it!

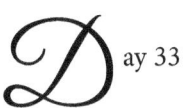 ay 33

DID you know that your heart wants you to brag? This is the case because your heart is the host of your soul being and your soul being is definitely all about brag, bragging, and nothing less, because your soul being is the biggest fan of you. So, if your heart is a bragging entity and your soul is its partner in crime, what's keeping you from boasting about yourself in the highest form ever? Why is such a loving thing like bragging so hard for you? Without digging deep into the reasons and issues - since I only asked for inspirational purposes - what gloating show will you gift yourself today? Could a bragging trot do the trick?

___

Bragging - Because you're worth it!

 ay 34

IN A PERFECT WORLD of braggers - also called shiners because they shine their light bright no matter what - there are no mistakes only gifts, experiences, energies, expansions, calibrations, and learning opportunities. Are you a bragger by now? Is your perfect world full of these gifts—even if at first they seem like mistakes?

Bragging - Because you're worth it!

 ay 35

EARLY ON TRAINED braggers like you - just think of when you were a diaper baby and all there was for you, was YOU - love to pretend to ride through life on their high horses—proud and tall on a glorious stallion. But why does it have to be pretend, when in reality it is your truth and you want this to be your reality? I say, stop acting like it isn't so and start bragging your way back to how you started out—a boasting youngling who was happy to make it all about yourself.

Bragging - Because you're worth it!

 ay 36

BRAGGING HELPS you clarify everything about yourself and your life because either your boasting makes you feel higher, meaning that you are on point with what you want and who you are—or it does not feel good, indicating that your direction is misaligned or your self-love is out of whack. That is clarity!

Bragging - Because you're worth it!

 ay 37

BRAGGING DOES NOT ALWAYS MEAN SHOUTING from the top of your lungs about how cool you are, nor does it mean being the life of every party. Many times all it means, is a deep inner relaxation and knowing that you are perfect the way you are and deserve to feel amazing. So fit the desired bragging-style to your daily needs, or split-second wishes! That way you are in heaven with yourself and in sync with taking care of yourself—giving you fuel to brag even more, hence today's invitation, "I know how to give myself the best of the best!"

Bragging - Because you're worth it!

 ay 38

SENSE YOUR ENERGY! Are you small or big, hiding or exposing, smiling or stern, heavy or light, happy or unhappy? In order to have a good-feeling boasting time, it's important to learn to read your energetic essence and know how to shift into a good-feeling state if you are not, because great bragging asks for being in an aligned state. How are you reading yourself right now? Are you aligned or not? Make this a daily, if not hourly, practice!

Bragging - Because you're worth it!

ay 39

WHEN WAS the last time you bragged about yourself? Yesterday? Well, that is too long ago. An hour ago? Also far too much time that has passed. Just a second ago? That's better, but why leave time in between? Go, bragger hero, go! Keep it up!

Bragging - Because you're worth it!

 ay 40

BRAGGERS LOVE TO HAVE FUN, and to play lightheartedly with life and all that is there to be in bliss with. Go on, natural bragger, you have not un-learned to play nor are you not good at bragging. You just tuned it out a little! How will you play and brag, and brag and play, all day long?

___

Bragging - Because you're worth it!

 Day 41

As a bragging being you will witness synchronicity all the time, because being over-the-top in love with yourself is a guaranteed alignment with your inner being, which always knows what your perfect next - and even next-er - step is for you. You see, bragging has all kinds of perks for you! What wonderful signs of being on your perfect path are you noticing?

_____
_____
_____
_____
_____
_____
_____
_____
_____
_____
_____
_____
_____
_____
_____
_____
_____
_____
_____
_____

Bragging - Because you're worth it!

 Day 42

A BRAGGING HEART MOVES MOUNTAINS, because its essence is of an unwilling-ness to budge to anything that is not loving towards you. Your heart also creates the strongest energy there is, your love, and is the host of your soul being—your biggest and most knowing part of you. Feel your bragging heart; what is it saying for you, about you, to you, and with you?

___

Bragging - Because you're worth it!

 ay 43

A BRAGGING brain thinks gloating thoughts and creates a boastingly powerful energy for you to BE and live in—feel these powerful words carrying such highly regarded wisdom! How can you nourish your brain into more bragging—is it through a bragger-list outlining what there is to brag about? How will you create a more gloating thinking style—one that fits your new bragging brain? When is it time for you to BE and live more of your new bragging you? Is now a perfect time? Please say, "Yes!"

Bragging - Because you're worth it!

ay 44

A BRAGGING nose and tastebuds are willing to smell and taste whatever is out there and are also very sure to loudly measure up and signal when something seems on the pungent side. Is there anything that smells or tastes weird to you, yet that you feel obligated to tolerate? "No more," I say. Be brave and follow the lead of your bragging senses that enjoy what's heavenly and are clear when something isn't. You owe it to yourself, bragger!

___

Bragging - Because you're worth it!

 ay 45

A BRAGGING body - that might seem odd at first, but is it really? - shows up physically as an undying force of life, being alive, and vividness—no matter the size, shape, or look. It carries itself as a proud, secure, and knowing energy—again, no matter the circumstances. Think about it, the fact that you are a body - besides being a mind, soul, and consciousness - is enough to dance in a bragging style. Are you hip with that?

Bragging - Because you're worth it!

 Day 46

BRAGGING eyes glow far and wide and are determined to enchant you with what they see and the light they spread—mesmerizing and capable of bragging without words! Go look into a mirror, right now. Are your eyes gloating from deep inside? Yes? Then you are good to go! If not—it's time to practice, and what better time than to start shining your pupils now? Light them up, bragger!

Bragging - Because you're worth it!

 ay 47

BRAGGING EARS ARE AWARE, alert, and ready to hear all of the positive and happy stuff that is out there—but also in you. They sift through the junk and get straight into the bragging state of, "I hear the good stuff!" I say, fill your whole being with all the glory that you hear and go on to hear even more wonderful news, just to turn around and brag about that too.

Bragging - Because you're worth it!

 Day 48

A BRAGGING soul is like a bragging mother—always has your back, guides you to your wellbeing, loves you unconditionally, and can't stop talking or gushing about who they love to gloat about: You!!! Why not focus on this bragging inner you that knows exactly how much worth, deserving of, lovable, intelligent, abundant, successful, unique, special, beautiful, and wonderful you are? Come on bragger, let yourself be showered by it!

Bragging - Because you're worth it!

 ay 49

Do you think a superhero is a natural bragger—the way they carry themselves, what they can do and are capable of, and how everyone sees them? I hopefully sense a "Yes!"

What's not to say that you are a superhero too? You carry yourself physically and as a whole being—body, mind, soul, and consciousness. You are capable of anything and because of that can do anything—especially with the help of your inner being and the universe. Most people see beyond the small little *here's* and *there's* that you don't like about yourself and instead, they see your champion you—making you a true superhero! How will you manage such a bragging fact more often?

_____
_____
_____
_____
_____
_____
_____
_____
_____
_____
_____
_____
_____
_____
_____
_____

Bragging - Because you're worth it!

 ay 50

BRAGGING WORDS ARE UPLIFTING, strengthening, energizing, heightening, and of a gushing nature. Anything of lesser value that is being said is not bragging, shifting you immediately into a lower frequency—one in which a true bragger doesn't want to be. Go on, write your bragging word list, then use them often and update it constantly.

_____
_____
_____
_____
_____
_____
_____
_____
_____
_____
_____
_____
_____
_____
_____
_____
_____
_____
_____
_____
_____

Bragging - Because you're worth it!

 ay 51

IT TAKES a little practice to learn the art of bragging! You might ask "Why is it an art?" First of all, it's unique to you since there is only one of YOU, and only you can create your bragger life. It also involves your creativity to keep it uplifting and fun, and asks for your passion of being in love with yourself. Plus, there are no limits - just like with art - to how incredible of a life you can be inspired to live. It really is an artful lifestyle, your gloating ways! What would your bragger-art-piece look like? What colors, grand-ness, and originality? Now go ahead and match your life to that!

___

Bragging - Because you're worth it!

 ay 52

BRAGGING about yourself asks for a bit of bravery, and as we have already covered before, a lot of self love. But it also initiates your courage to speak highly of yourself, your boldness to unconditionally be proud of yourself, your fearlessness to be you without a spec of others in the mix, your lionhearted-ness to go for what you want, your daring-ness to say "No!" when it's necessary for you, and your heroic-ness to not over-help others and instead, give only what's healthy for you. Bragging really brings out the best in you! How will you align with your limitless brave-heart?

Bragging - Because you're worth it!

 ay 53

Let's get a bit banana-listic here! If you would put a worth on the different parts of you, how many bananas would each part be? Be generous with your bananas here—1 is of lesser value than 1000. For example: your eyes, feet, organs, your brain and thoughts, your inner being, your whole you—what is your added up banana-value? Go on, list your parts, give them value, and add up all your bananas. Then be amazed how fruiticious you are and go bananas - and brag - about your worth!

_____
_____
_____
_____
_____
_____
_____
_____
_____
_____
_____
_____
_____
_____
_____
_____
_____
_____

Bragging - Because you're worth it!

 ay 54

WHAT IN YOUR LIFE, that has just happened, could you brag about to yourself, others, to nature, or to the sky? Go on, what are you waiting for? Gloat, wonderful being, gloat!

Bragging - Because you're worth it!

 ay 55

BRAGGING yourself back into alignment with who you really are when you catch yourself being out of whack is the biggest gift that you can give to yourself—but also to your surroundings. Why? Because when you are out of alignment, you are not showing up as the best you that you can be, whereas when you are in your alignment - then combine that with your bragging self - you are an unstoppable and ultimate bright light. What is your bragger-plan—just in case you need it?

___
___
___
___
___
___
___
___
___
___
___
___
___
___
___
___
___
___

Bragging - Because you're worth it!

 ay 56

Since bragging is in direct alignment with who you really are - a whole being that loves to have fun - it's only natural that laughter and jokes are part of a bragging life style. How will you brag more—ahem, laugh and joke more?

___

Bragging - Because you're worth it!

ay 57

BRAGGING CAN BE A VERY SILENT, dense, and calm activity—but also a loud and shouting one. Depending on the day, situation, and your needs, it is of utmost value to stay flexible and choose the fitting kind of gushing newly, and over and over. It's important to remember that aligned gloating - being *ONE* with your inner being - is powerful, whereas un-alignment feels gunky. What is your flair for today? Choose it like you would select the perfect clothing for the day.

Bragging - Because you're worth it!

ay 58

BRAGGING IS an inside job first and foremost—as we already covered. It is best done for yourself at the start so you learn to breathe into it and also know how good it feels and how much joy it can be. Then, once you are rooted in it and you have got the hang of it, you can happily take a stroll and show your bragging-self to the world. When asking your inner you, what is it telling you to brag about right now—in stillness first, and then in loudness after?

___

Bragging - Because you're worth it!

 ay 59

TAKE THE SUN, moon, stars, the sky, space or a spaceship, race car or bicycle, fighter jet or bald eagle, elephant or a billion year old tree. They all have one thing in common, they are a powerful energy—one that knows what to do, what it wants, and certainly can't be overlooked. Bragging essences, all showing up in different ways! What is your bragging essence right now? I know it is huge—but is it loud, soft, dense, bold, or regal? Remember, you change all the time and your bragging ways want to do the same, so stay in tune!

Bragging - Because you're worth it!

 ay 60

Do you think that a relaxed person, chilling and indulging with a smile into the knowing that they are deserving to take wonderful breaks, is of a bragging nature? I think so! You have to be sure about yourself and your life, and be self-loving and aligned to make relaxation happen—it's like saying, "I know that I want to take this time—so I take it!" That's a bragging state, so yes, relaxing means that you are a successful bragger. How will you chillax more often?

_____
_____
_____
_____
_____
_____
_____
_____
_____
_____
_____
_____
_____
_____
_____
_____
_____

Bragging - Because you're worth it!

 ay 61

BRAGGING lifts the whole world into a higher state—because the more you brag, the more others can, will, or are invited to brag too. It's like the louder one gets when in a crowd, the louder the crowd gets. So keep bragging, and know that you are a phenomenal uplifter for yourself but also for others. Who is going to get some of your magic today, and what type of bliss can you brag about more?

___

Bragging - Because you're worth it!

 ay 62

GETTING to know yourself and your skills, joys, preferences, and dreams without taking your focus of being aligned with your magic, means that you know exactly what to brag about. Remember, you have many strong points so don't stiff yourself here. After all, this is a journal about bragging big, and then even bigger. The signals you will give out by doing so are, "I get myself, and through that, I get you too!" "I support myself, so I can support you too!"—because what you do for yourself, you can easily do for others as well. Bragging really does accomplish a lot! Your talent-sheet please!

___

Bragging - Because you're worth it!

 ay 63

ARE you looking for a new job, new or more love, a new location to live, inspirations for what to do next, more money, success, abundance, or a new fulfillment of any kind? How can you shift and lift yourself into a high-for-life frequency where all those new desires are ready to be called into existence? You guessed right! By bragging about anything and everything that you can think of—yourself, your surroundings, and even others. It goes something like this: "This day is the best day ever!" "I am worthy of the best of the best!" "My surroundings are more beautiful than ever!" "These people are all superheroes!" Those phrases are all great uplifters to fly high and in the same frequency of your dreams. Try it; what bragging sayings can you come up with? Say and feel them often!

___

Bragging - Because you're worth it!

 ay 64

It's so easy to be you and life is so easy to live! Let me give you a visual. You walk down the street and a flower waves its scent at you; you drive in your car and the lines on the street show how alignment works; food naturally awakens a deliciousness in you, children remind you to laugh and play, the sky initiates an openness you can choose to latch onto, and water helps you feel the energy of flow. Must I go on? Consciously and mindfully take advantage of this given easiness and quit making it so hard! Then, start bragging about your easy journey that you are here to enjoy!

Bragging - Because you're worth it!

 Day 65

THERE IS ALWAYS MORE, higher, better, healthier, happier, and a superior fit! Think about it—until you die there is always the possibility of more. Why don't you grab that fact and start choosing more, better, and higher without ever stopping? Is it because of old beliefs and habits—thinking that you are being too demanding or that there is not enough? Life certainly does not think that, since it is an energy of abundance, plentifulness, and limitlessness. How will you align with the *more* that you and your life are? When will you start bragging about that *more*—to make it come true and manifest its way into your awareness?

Bragging - Because you're worth it!

 ay 66

DO YOU REALLY MEAN IT—TO live your best life ever? Are you really committed to doing anything necessary to experience the time of your life? I hear a "Yes!" Perfect. That means you need to stop whatever you are doing—to breathe, relax, smile, and become an enjoyer, then get into bragging about how much fun you are having. Are you still with me here, and are you willing to make your creative list of how you will get all this bliss going? I say, don't waste any more split seconds!

___

Bragging - Because you're worth it!

 ay 67

OK, this might seem out of the ordinary but go with it please! Start dancing through your day while singing, "I AM the best in the world!" "I am the smartest around!" "I am the most beautiful that has ever lived!" "I am THE most important person there IS!"

It's key that you don't think too hard here, and to not let your mind and old beliefs get in the way—after all, your singing is the truth because for YOU, you really are the best, smartest, most beautiful, and most important person ever. Nobody else is capable of taking your place! Sing and dance, bragger!

Bragging - Because you're worth it!

 ay 68

MANY TIMES we brag about things, situations, or people that we don't want in our life—by talking about it. Think about it, we even put time aside to tell another person: "Meet me then and there and I'll tell you all about it." This highlights that bragging can go either way—uplifting or down-pulling. Question is, what downer-gloating will you refrain from and what could be the uplifting and extraordinary side of things?

___

Bragging - Because you're worth it!

Day 69

BRAGGING IS the most natural thing to do - just think of the bragging event your birth was and how naturally you pulled it off - unless you are letting your old rugged beliefs and habits of "never brag about yourself because that means you are full of yourself" get in the way. But no worries, all you need is a little of re-learning and some practice to get back in the swing of gloating. How will you go *au naturelle* again and give up the fight against who you really are?

Bragging - Because you're worth it!

Day 70

THINK of watching a blah movie with blah acting. Now, imagine that same movie being taken over the top by amazing animation and actors who go all in with their expressions and their acting. It's a whole different story! A life without bragging is a blah life with a blah actor—but wow, when you put your bragging to the test, your show becomes alive and incredibly energized. How will you activate your vivid magic and show up as THE only one who can make this time amazing?

Bragging - Because you're worth it!

ay 71

ARE you walking in a slouching way or are you trotting with pride and as tall as can be—honored to BE you? Sagging has the energetic value of lower, lesser, and maybe even exhausted, whereas the value of raised is the equivalent of powerful, limitless, but also being sure about who you are and in a bragging way. How can you focus on walking like you mean it more often? Is it by bragging your way into alignment, then enjoying a high-for-life skip?

Bragging - Because you're worth it!

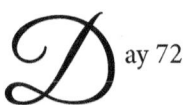

Day 72

WHEN BEING of a bragging kind you also attract the bragging kind, and we all know that whom you surround yourself with matters immensely for your sanity, as well as your emotional, physical - and also your energetic - health. What kind are you right now, and is it what you would enjoy in your outer world? If you are happy, keep bragging ahead. If not, then without changing anything outside of you, shift yourself to BE and live as your best bragging you—and see the effect for yourself.

Bragging - Because you're worth it!

 ay 73

WHAT IS your biggest hurdle to be a daily bragger and feel good while you're at it? Is it that it's new—which is not true since you were quite the bragger from the start, as we already covered? Is it because others are not self-gloaters? How do you truly know if that's the case—or if they're just waiting for you to lead the bragging-way? Is it because you think that bragging is wrong? Well, that old hat is even more wrong, since being full of yourself is an act of self-love and self-knowing. So what is it? List, please, and then have some bragging fun to blow these troubles to kingdom come!

Bragging - Because you're worth it!

ay 74

ONCE YOU ARE ACCUSTOMED to your new bragging life you will soon fall in love with the feeling that there is only one YOU—even if in your mind you already knew that fact, the feeling is what we are wanting to focus on here. How does it feel to know such a glorious truth—that you are such a unique essence and that there will never be another you? I hope you feel your importance here and trust that you will brag about it in overflow.

Bragging - Because you're worth it!

 ay 75

TO BE a cool and successful bragger you must choose to crack a smile over starting the biggest fight of your life, or at least you must try to make a conscious choice of which one is better in the actual moment. Usually a glowing bragger has more power than a mad gloater since flashing your teeth with a wide grin is more in alignment with who you really are, given, that sometimes being angry wins the argument—so choose wisely!

Bragging - Because you're worth it!

 ay 76

WHEN YOU BRAG, you open up; when you are open, you allow; when you allow, you receive; and when you receive, you hold your thrilling life and your dear manifestations in your hands—and as a result, your happiness speaks wonders. What are you waiting for? Keep bragging, and then gloat even more!

___

Bragging - Because you're worth it!

Day 77

WHAT RIGHT NOW WOULD, could, or will get you into a bragging state? Seriously, ask yourself this question every hour to keep your gushing state going. Then take your instructions as law to follow and do what you need to do, so that anything less than bragging about yourself is not on your horizon. Maybe a bragger alarm or reminder would do here?

Bragging - Because you're worth it!

 Day 78

WHAT IS A BRAGGING cheese to you—one that is boldly stinky with exquisite mold or one that is genuinely milky with flower petals on the rind? How about bold chocolate? Would you rather think dark with barely any sweetness, or does milk with caramel inside come to mind? And what about a meal; what is a bold dish for you? You get the point of this exercise and hopefully also the meaning that a bragging essence comes in many different shapes, sizes, and ways, and also changes all the time. How can you choose aligned bragger food, and also gloating experiences, all day long?

Bragging - Because you're worth it!

 ay 79

START A BRAGGER club or create a bragger group, talk about bragging with excitement, write a bragger blog, play a bragger game, watch a bragger show, practice a bragger sport—whatever you do, make sure to shift your whole life's affairs into being bragger activities, and say "so-long," to all else. Why? Because that is what you want more of in life—that unlimited amazingness! Go on, make your battle plan to have it your way, and ban anything that's of a lower value from your schedule.

Bragging - Because you're worth it!

Day 80

WHEN YOU ACCOMPLISH something great and you are holding the joy and glory in for yourself it can create goodness, but only if your inner being says, "It's aligned to keep this to myself." If you keep things under wraps because of how others might react, it would be better to jump over that hoop and let loose with bragging hugely because that will override your old ways of holding yourself back—shifting you into your wonderful alignment with who you really are. Plus, if you stay silent, nothing changes nor is anything old being cleansed out—not to mention the missed opportunity to celebrate yourself.

Bragging - Because you're worth it!

Day 81

Your dreams, wishes, desires, and also your passions are nothing else than your bragger-genie saying, "Hey, I am bold enough to want and have that, because I know that I deserve it and it feels rightly good for me!" So what is it that you so dearly want—what's your hold-back to get it? Make your genie statements!

_____
_____
_____
_____
_____
_____
_____
_____
_____
_____
_____
_____
_____
_____
_____
_____
_____
_____
_____
_____

Bragging - Because you're worth it!

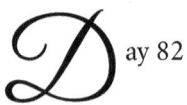 ay 82

IF YOU COULD SIT on a cloud and in the nothingness of the sky, what proudness would you shout out from the top of your lungs? Go on, nobody can hear you up there. You are safe and private, so what would you shout? I truly hope you are going braggerlistic here!

___

Bragging - Because you're worth it!

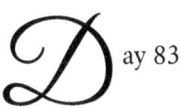

Day 83

BRAGGERS DON'T DWELL on old stuff, unfitting things, or out-of-sync people—instead, they are too busy bragging about themselves and their lives, so much so that they might not even notice those impurifications around them. Think about it; no more focusing on what you don't like because you are living a lifestyle that supports noticing what you do like. What a life! That is what becoming a diligent gloater will do for you. Are you still having any reservations about such a beautiful lifestyle?

___

Bragging - Because you're worth it!

 ay 84

IF YOU EVER DREAMT OF a wonderland where magic is always present you are not that far off from where you stand right now. Promise!

- For one, Earth is a wonderland, for sure!
- For two, you are magic, which is also a given!

So all that is really left for you to figure out is:

- What, on earth, do you sense as wonders—is it nature, cities, possibilities, or manifestations?
- What in, on, and as you is magic? Easy, since you have plenty of parts to choose from; your body, mind, soul, and consciousness.

Time to brag!

___
___
___
___
___
___
___
___
___
___
___

Bragging - Because you're worth it!

 ay 85

As I sit here writing this book, I see you as your huge mountainous bragging you—as a sure, bold, knowing, aligned, happy, successful, healthy, and abundant being. What a sight! Now, if I can see you that way, you surely can find a way to see yourself that way too and latch onto this wonderful truth of yours! How does that feel? What do you see in yourself? How powerful are you, and what are you going to do, now that you have realized your worth and value? Are you bragging about yourself yet?

___

Bragging - Because you're worth it!

 ay 86

You are so much worth and so much worth is you! In truth it's such an overwhelmingly obvious amount that if I would not know any better, I'd say that it's unbelievably crazy that I even have to convince you of such a fact. Let's fix that right now! Make your "I am worth it!" list! Gush, bragger, gush!

_____
_____
_____
_____
_____
_____
_____
_____
_____
_____
_____
_____
_____
_____
_____
_____
_____
_____
_____
_____
_____
_____
_____
_____

Bragging - Because you're worth it!

 ay 87

IMAGINE you own the most gorgeous mansion ever—one that you designed and built yourself. Some magazine wants to write about your mansion and come take pictures. With excitement, you say yes! The day has come, you start bragging about the mansion, showing room by room, while gushing about all the features there are. You are literally glowing with pride as the owner. Then, the magazine asks spontaneously about an interview with - and about - you as the builder. You decline, because you don't want to brag about yourself. That is how most people live—comfortably bragging about anything else but themselves, when all along that's really all there is to brag about. I say, go all into your bragging-business; the one that's all about you!

___

Bragging - Because you're worth it!

 ay 88

EVEN A BRAGGER NEEDS to un-brag sometimes. What's your cosy resting place; how does it look and feel, and what sounds relax you the most? There, you just created another bragging vision for yourself—and if you feel like it, let others hear all about it.

Bragging - Because you're worth it!

ay 89

WHAT's the most bragging word you can find? How about the most bragging color you would choose? Or the most bragging feeling there is? Do you have a most bragging taste, smell, or sound? What about your most bragging vision? "Tell me all about your deepest boasting, you bragger, you!" says your *in-love-with-you* journal!

Bragging - Because you're worth it!

 ay 90

Never mix your wonderful bragging with any gloating out there that does not feel good, and is not yours! Never! Why? This gunks your clean bragger pipe up and blocks the flow of your freely gained gusher life—making you stop bragging because it's of an un-well feeling nature. Stay aligned in your pure bragger lane at all times!

Bragging - Because you're worth it!

* * *

Ready to continue on your self-growth path? Get the next journal in this series: ***Of Course! Because why wait...***

BONUS

Because hey, nobody ever wants the goodness to end.

Keep on bragging—it really suits you!

# Day 91

THROUGH YOUR BRAGGER HEART AND coming from your truth-saying lips, repeat after me, "I am me and they are they—and I stay me even when they are they!" Can you be alert enough to stays focused on yourself, and only on yourself—no exceptions? Why? Because too much peeking left or right is not good for your bragging self. How will you stay focused on you?

Bragging - Because you're worth it!

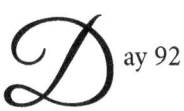 Day 92

You are a limitless bragger! At least as your energetic you, living in your physical body and experiencing physicality—your inner being always has more to brag about. Knowing that, are you putting a cap onto your bragger abilities because you live with the old belief of being limited? I say, cut it out!

Bragging - Because you're worth it!

ay 93

CAN BRAGGERS ALSO BE NAY-SAYERS, negative-ers, and down-ers? Yes they can—but it's bragging into an un-well direction and you don't want to be part of it. Instead, jump ship! Then steer away - alone if you must - to get to shore where aligned bragging that fits your style is happening. The disaligned? Let them be.

Bragging - Because you're worth it!

 ay 94

As the bragger that you are, do you take enough time to get better at your gloating-craft? Because just like everything else, it takes time to become the best of the best—while also feeling and believing in yourself that you are the strongest ever. How are you going to make time for gushing?

___

Bragging - Because you're worth it!

 ay 95

THINK about the gloating power of the universe inviting you, as a bragger yourself, to co-create and have the most thrilling fun while at it! Things can't get any more exciting than that! Go on, how does that feel? What are you going to do - or stop doing - while being in such a strong partnership?

___

Bragging - Because you're worth it!

AND NOW IT'S YOUR TURN!

The following are your magical pages to become your own unstoppable bragger-boss!

I'm counting on you to go full-of-yourself here!

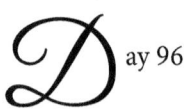 ay 96

BRAGGING IS COOL BECAUSE...

Bragging - Because you're worth it!

# Day 97

BRAGGING FEELS GOOD BECAUSE…

Bragging - Because you're worth it!

# Day 98

BRAGGING MAKES ME HAPPY BECAUSE...

___

Bragging - Because you're worth it!

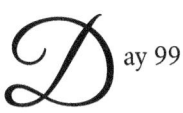 Day 99

BRAGGING IS HEALTHY BECAUSE…

Bragging - Because you're worth it!

 ay 100

BRAGGING IS the best ever because…

___

Bragging - Because you're worth it!

* * *

Don't forget to leave a review on Amazon.com and Goodreads.com as soon as you can, as your kind feedback helps other readers find my books easier. Thank you!

ALSO BY JACQUELINE PIRTLE

365 Days of Happiness

Because happiness is a piece of cake!

This passage book invites you to create a daily habit to live your every day joy, and is the parent companion to *365 Days of Happiness*, the journal workbook.

* * *

365 Days of Happiness - Special Edition

Because happiness is a piece of cake

This beautiful Special Edition of the bestseller *365 Days of Happiness: Because happiness is a piece of cake* has room for your notes after every daily passage.

* * *

365 Days of Happiness - Journal Workbook

Because happiness is a piece of cake

This enlightening journal workbook is your daily tool to create a habit of living your every day bliss, and is the companion to *365 Days of Happiness: Because happiness is a piece of cake*.

* * *

Life IS Beautiful - Here's to New Beginnings

If you like digging deeper into the meaning of life and are inspired by spirituality, then you'll love Jacqueline's effective teachings.

* * *

Parenting Through the Eyes of Lollipops

A Guide to Conscious Parenting

If you like harmony at home and laughter in the house, then you'll love Jacqueline's inspirational methods.

* * *

What it Means to BE a Woman

And Yes! Women do Poop!

If you like to live free, empowered, and want to decide for yourself, then you'll love Jacqueline's liberating ways.

* * *

Life-changing Journals

What. If. - Turning your IFs into it IS!

Open - Where it all starts!

To BE and Live - The reason you are here!

High for Life - The best case scenario!

Of course - Because why wait!

Every journal comes in two lengths:

A 30 day journal

A 90 day journal - The Extended Edition

If you like being in charge of your own life, turning your dreams into reality, enjoy journaling, and want to squeeze the most out of your time, then you'll love Jacqueline's uplifting teachings.

ABOUT THE AUTHOR

Bestselling author, podcaster, and holistic practitioner, Jacqueline Pirtle, has twenty-four years of experience helping thousands of clients discover their own happiness. Jacqueline is the owner of *FreakyHealer* and has shared her solid teachings through her podcast **The Daily Freak**, sessions, workshops, presentations, and books with clients all over the world. She holds international degrees in holistic health and natural living. Her effective healing work has been featured in print and online magazines, podcasts, radio shows, on TV, and in the documentary *The Overly Emotional Child by Learning Success*, available on Amazon Prime.

For any questions you might have, to sign up for Jacqueline's newsletter, and for more information on whatever else she is up to, visit www.freakyhealer.com and her social media accounts @freakyhealer.

www.ingramcontent.com/pod-product-compliance
Lightning Source LLC
Chambersburg PA
CBHW071420070526
44578CB00003B/629